THROUGH THEIR EYES

A WHOLE NEW WORLD

Edited By Lynsey Evans

First published in Great Britain in 2024 by:

Young Writers
Remus House
Coltsfoot Drive
Peterborough
PE2 9BF
Telephone: 01733 890066
Website: www.youngwriters.co.uk

All Rights Reserved
Book Design by Ashley Janson
© Copyright Contributors 2024
Softback ISBN 978-1-83565-496-5
Printed and bound in the UK by BookPrintingUK
Website: www.bookprintinguk.com
YB0592V

FOREWORD

Since 1991, here at Young Writers we have celebrated the awesome power of creative writing, especially in young adults, where it can serve as a vital method of expressing strong (and sometimes difficult) emotions, a conduit to develop empathy, and a safe, non-judgemental place to explore one's own place in the world. With every poem we see the effort and thought that each pupil published in this book has put into their work and by creating this anthology we hope to encourage them further with the ultimate goal of sparking a life-long love of writing.

Through Their Eyes challenged young writers to open their minds and pen bold, powerful poems from the points-of-view of any person or concept they could imagine – from celebrities and politicians to animals and inanimate objects, or even just to give us a glimpse of the world as they experience it. The result is this fierce collection of poetry that by turns questions injustice, imagines the innermost thoughts of influential figures or simply has fun.

The nature of the topic means that contentious or controversial figures may have been chosen as the narrators, and as such some poems may contain views or thoughts that, although may represent those of the person being written about, by no means reflect the opinions or feelings of either the author or us here at Young Writers.

We encourage young writers to express themselves and address subjects that matter to them, which sometimes means writing about sensitive or difficult topics. If you have been affected by any issues raised in this book, details on where to find help can be found at *www.youngwriters.co.uk/info/other/contact-lines*

CONTENTS

Al-Islah Girls' High School, Blackburn

Hijjah Khalid (15)	1
Aisha Hussain (14)	2
Iqra Ahmed (15)	4
Khadija Shanzay (13)	6
Aamna Zafar (16)	8
Sumaiyah Chhiboo (15)	9
Rahma Amhar (13)	10
Amina Torofdar (14)	11
Imaan Zahra Farid (17)	12
Hidayah Sadiq (13)	13
Sanaa Ali (15)	14
Hafsah Mulla (13)	15
Mehak Hussain Kousar (15)	16
Juwayriyah Hussain (13)	17
Zahra Hussain (12)	18
Aroush Mudassir (13)	19
Inaya Qadri Baciu (13)	20
Rukhma Shakeel (15)	21
Zaynab Vepari (13)	22
Seerat Fatima (12)	23
Eshal Sheikh Sadique (13)	24
Umamah Khan (14)	25
Safiyyah Mulla (13)	26

All Saints' Catholic Academy, Mansfield

Diya Dixon (13)	27
Monika Wojtas (12)	28
Hafsa Kebbeh (13)	31
Daniel Dixon (13)	32
Heidi Brickles (12)	33
Henry Bailey (14)	34

Tristan Tennyson (13)	35
Ellie Spier (15)	36
Cora Lilleyman (13)	37
Ruby-Leigh Bettles (13)	38
Kathryn Saunders (12)	39

Cathkin High School, Cambuslang

Madeleine Whyte (15)	40

Cleeve School, Cheltenham

Chloe Kite	41

Colfe's School, Lee

Zoe Zimmermann (12)	44
Justin Gao (11)	45
Charlotte Foster (11)	46
Alecsia Sydorowitz (12)	47
Ifijen Ifebajo (12)	48

Cowley Academy, Spalding

Enija Butane (12)	49

Davenies School, Beaconsfield

Sebastian Shelton (12)	50
Harris Lafferty (12)	53

Davison CE High School For Girls, Worthing

Alice Wilson (13)	54

Dyke House Academy, Hartlepool

Annabelle Hedley-Price (13)	56
Jude Jones (11)	58

Elizabeth Woodville School, Deanshanger

Ava-Jade Charles (12)	59
Ava Hardwick (11)	60
Oliver B (12)	62
Isabel Smith (12)	63
Ethan Davies (12)	64
Millie Hewitt (12)	65
Jay Knox (11)	66
Chloe Seath (12)	67
Alfie Dunn (12)	68
Ellie Sargent (12)	69
Lily Tomlin (11)	70
Aimee Kerr (12)	71
Fleur Westwood (11)	72
Harry Johnson (11)	73
Finley Pearce (11)	74
William Watson (12)	75
Neve Binns (11)	76
Toby Hill (13)	77
Ella Borton-Berry (12)	78
Ben Margiotta (13)	79
Liam Owens (12)	80
Gabriel Brown (13)	81
Dillan-Eric Staig (11)	82
Erin Bell (11)	83
Francis Gjinushi (11)	84
Lacey Elliott (11)	85

Great Sankey High School, Great Sankey

Olive Bryan (12)	86

Hanley Castle High School, Hanley Castle

Ruby McAlpine (12)	87
Luke Hastings (12)	88
Mireille Shaw (11)	90
Alex Allen-Goble (11)	92
Megan Down (14)	94
Ben Sharp (11)	96
Zara Rudd (11)	97
Ruben Fowler (13)	98
Audrey-Lillian Price (13)	100
Imogen Betteridge (13)	102
Oscar Keeble-Buckle (11)	105
Joshua Davis (13)	106
Travis Hammill (13)	108
Rupert Millikin (12)	110
Harry Kwiecien (12)	111
Connor McNamara (12)	112
Olive Roberts (12)	114
Lily Crook (12)	115
Archie Wills (11)	116
Bessie Tame (12)	117
Tom Smallpage (12)	118
Millie Thomas (12)	119
Daisy Ridsdale (12)	120
Teddy Surman (12)	122
Bonnie Bowness (11)	123
Elias Goff (11)	124
Jamie Collins (11)	125
Daisy Helsby (14)	126
River Yeates (13)	127
Holly Longhi (11)	128
Freya Harris (12)	129
Molly Widdrington (13)	130
Jack Harris (11)	131
George Potter (11)	132
Viktoria Dimitrova (13)	133
Aiden Booth	134
Ava Hockett (12)	135
Frederick Hanson (12)	136
James Kelly (11)	137
Imogen Clements (13)	138
Megan Jones (13)	139

Name	Number
Mason Reed-Darby (13)	140
Lilly Morgan (12)	141
Teddy Hickman (12)	142
Sophie Brown (13)	143
Ronia Fisher (12)	144
Emily Evans (12)	145
Ellie George (13)	146
Eva Koenig (12)	147
Zach Morgan (11)	148
Isabella Smith (11)	149
Issy Kinghorn (12)	150
Mia Walker-Hobday (12)	151
Luca Colledge (11)	152
Lucia Hanson (13)	153
Peter Badger (12)	154
Imogen Dobson (11)	155
Scarlett Causon (12)	156
Jack Horton (12)	157
Harry March (11)	158
Toby Lee (12)	159
Alfie Sladen (12)	160
Jacob Eastwood (12)	161
Bethan Bowdrey (12)	162
Eoin Hands (13)	163
Izzy Kingston-Schleider (12)	164
Lilly Fisher (13)	165
Alana Robinson (12)	166
Rosie Roberts (13)	167
Charlie Avery-Rule (13)	168
Jack Claridge (13)	169
Freya Jones (13)	170
Jack Barker (12)	171
Rowan Marchant (13)	172
Faith Edmundson (12)	173
Jenson Perris (11)	174
Summer Adams (11)	175
Joel Thomas (11)	176
Abbie Riley (11)	177
Daisy Manning (11)	178
Jozlyn Connor (13)	179
Laila Clarke (13)	180
Maddie Bracewell-Hutton (13)	181
Bailey Matthews (12)	182
Lottie Dorkings (11)	183
Aiden Wilson (12)	184
Millie Hope Myers-Cooksey (13)	185
Bibi Rozier (13)	186
Harry Reed-Darby (12)	187
Zay Singh-Doyle (11)	188
Finley Ellis (12)	189
Samuel Walker (14)	190
Zack Jones (12)	191
Louis Hargreaves (12)	192
Kipras Jarmalavicius (11)	193
Ethan Baker (12)	194

THE
POEMS

Seeing The Dark Night In The Rain (Through Her Eyes)

It was a dark and stormy night,
The sounds of raindrops in a silent place,
I was seeing the world through her eyes.
I heard the smooth voice of an owl in the dark night,
It was black everywhere. It was full of darkness,
Nobody could hear my voice in the gloomy night, in the rain,
The bright moon was shining in the darkness,
I heard the sound of a wolf crying in the rain,
I was seeing the world through her eyes.
There was a shadow in that heavy rain,
Full of darkness, silence and blackness,
The soft raindrops fell on my face,
The fear was in my mind,
It was totally silent in the darkness, in the rain,
No sound except the raindrops,
It was cold and windy,
I heard the sound of leaves in the darkness, in the rain,
I was seeing the world through her eyes.
In the dark night, in the rain.

Hijjab Khalid (15)
Al-Islah Girls' High School, Blackburn

Orphaned

I'm lying in bed,
I hear a phone call,
A house has been bombed,
I'm scared,
Anxious and stressed,
Who is it? I wonder,
My dad barges in,
"Your granddad's house, it's been bombed."
A stifled sob,
It's my mother,
Where's she going?

Moments later...
Another phone call,
Who could it be now?
I get up to go see,
Dad picks it up before me,
As he puts the phone down,
His hand trembles,
An uncomfortable cry comes out of him,
I immediately understand,
Mum's been martyred,
A sob comes down my cheek.

In the middle of the night, I wake up,
To the sound of my baby sister's cry,
I get up to go say hi,

But when she sees me she cries,
Behind me, I hear a loud roar,
What's happening?
Boom! Boom!
I grab my sister,
And sprint out,
Behind me, my house,
My childhood home falls,
No! Dad's still in there,
I leave my sister with her bear,
I run to the rubble. "Dad! Dad!"
I scream at the top of my lungs,
I dig and dig till I find something,
My father's corpse,
An uncomfortable cry,
At that moment I realise
Me and my beautiful baby sister,
We are now orphans.

Aisha Hussain (14)
Al-Islah Girls' High School, Blackburn

Eyes Of Earth

I see everything,
Little do you know, I'm always watching,
I can see into all of your lives,
Your evening dinners and late-night drives.

I can see your struggle and writhing,
Your avid sense of fear rising,
The withering away of your day,
The sleepless nights on which you pray.

Every little thing I notice,
This life of yours is all but bliss,
But I shelter your pain and hold it in,
Yet you know not of your selfish sin.

You scar me with your dirt,
Do you think it doesn't hurt?
In your waters lies my blood,
Stained and tinted, still misunderstood.

You cut me down and use me,
Step on me and bruise me,
Open your eyes and see,
What it is that I can see.

You too will realise,
It is now too late to heed my cries,
For you are my steward but,
You care not.

What am I, that I can see all?
This so-called universe of yours.

You ask me mother, but you named me yourself.
I am your world, am I not?

Iqra Ahmed (15)
Al-Islah Girls' High School, Blackburn

Communication

She's a few years older than me,
Three years if you ask,
It was her mother who had found me,
While I was abandoned as an orphan.

I am unable to communicate with others,
I am resistant to physical touch,
I find discomfort from comfort,
And am isolated in the dark.

'Sociopath' she would say,
With the mind of a snake,
Since it's for her sake,
I decided not to be fake.

"You don't like people?"
Technically I do,
They're made of cells and atoms,
Which is what I enjoy.

"How about kids, babies?"
Those selfish creatures,
Wasting their tears,
And show their puppy eyes.

Sitting down with the lights off,
The whispers in my head,
Being heard from a mile away,
Taking indeed the better of me.

An isolated introvert,
Also seeming anti-social,
Even a sociopath to say,
But all have no mistake.

Khadija Shanzay (13)
Al-Islah Girls' High School, Blackburn

A Baby's Eyes

I'm new to this world, so fresh and so bright,
Everything's new, everything's a delight,
I see the world through my curious eyes,
Everything's a wonder, everything's a surprise.

I see the world with a sense of wonder,
Everything's new, everything's a thunder,
I see the world with a sense of glee,
Everything's perfect, everything's free.

I see the world with a sense of peace,
Everything's new, everything's a release,
I see the world with a sense of grace,
Everything's perfect, everything's in place.

I see the world with a sense of joy,
Everything's new, everything's a toy,
I see the world with a sense of love,
Everything's beautiful, everything's a dove.

Aamna Zafar (16)
Al-Islah Girls' High School, Blackburn

Through The Eyes Of A Child In A War Zone

In the war-torn land, through a child's eyes,
A tale of sorrow and longing, where hope often dies.
Among the ruins and rubble, their innocence fades,
A story unfolds, in the shadows it wades.

In their eyes I see a world torn apart.
They dream of peaceful skies,
But instead they witness destruction.

Through their eyes I witness a childhood lost.
Their places are destroyed,
Their laughter silenced by the sounds of bombs.

In a war-torn land, a tale unfolds,
Where stories of struggle and pain are told.
A place of conflict, where hearts are torn.

People pray for peace but it's hard to find,
As tensions rise and peace seems restricted,
Innocent lives affected, their dreams crushed.

Sumaiyah Chhiboo (15)
Al-Islah Girls' High School, Blackburn

Far Away Land

I'm six and all I hear are bombs repeated,
Is this how I'm supposed to be treated?
On the left I can see my mum packing our bag,
On the right my sister is crying with bombs exploding.
I just feel the world is imploding right on top of my head,
Lots of people on the ground, dead.

Wondering if this is the end,
Wondering if I did something to deserve this,
Wondering why they don't want peace,
Wondering why they want war instead.

Can't get any sleep,
Just hearing people scream day and night.
Looking up, the sky is grey,
Looking down, the ground is dark.

I wake up seeing the same story again and again.
Asking myself, is this how I live?

Rahma Amhar (13)
Al-Islah Girls' High School, Blackburn

Life's Tough

I wake up, my back bruised from the rough floor,
My fingers number from the icy air,

My living conditions,
Are unfair,

Time to find breakfast, I think with a moan,
A few messages pop up as I glance at my phone,

I beg on the streets, hoping for some food,
In an instant, I see something that changes my mood,

A rich couple walking around, enjoying their day,
Why, I used to be like you, I almost say,

But I'm aware I'm now like this,
Long gone are my days full of happiness and bliss,

And so I'm alone with a bag of my stuff,
With nothing but the good earth as my bed,
That's that - life's tough.

Amina Torofdar (14)
Al-Islah Girls' High School, Blackburn

My Angel Baby

As my eyes fall upon this girl
With beautiful hair, in soft curls
She looks at me, as though I am her world.

She has angelic looks, as if she is as pure as water
She is everything I need, my perfect daughter.

Her innocence shines like a glistening moon
And the time for sunrise will come so soon.

Her voice, in my ears, cries a tune
As though she is trying to heal a wound.

She is trying to heal the wound
That she did not make.

She is sweet and delicate, and very kind
She is the first thing that comes to my mind.

She is the pleasure of my existence
The purpose of my life.

Imaan Zahra Farid (17)
Al-Islah Girls' High School, Blackburn

A Shadow

The heavy waves crashed
and the sun shone bright.
The distant trees sighed
as the air grew tight.
Who knew this was the start of something
something that shouldn't be right?

A silence encroached near and near,
until we saw a shadow appear.
A man wearing nothing but black
and a hint of gold on his belt and hat.
His boots had hooks at the front and sides
and a watch of which was gold and bright.

He lowered his hand and wrapped it tightly
and curled his fingers round delightfully.
He raised his pistol and broadly grinned
and that was the last from Charlie Mind.

Hidayah Sadiq (13)
Al-Islah Girls' High School, Blackburn

Heartbroken

I was sleeping and woke up to a horrible bombing
Me and my family could smell smoke
I had a little baby brother who could barely breathe
I ran out of the house with my family
And we all went in different directions to get help
Two hours later we were all separated
My family were nowhere to be found
I was helpless, heartbroken and scared
I had nowhere to go
I had no clothes besides what I was wearing
No family and no food
The attack was so bad that my life almost went
The bomb came next to me
Then my life flashed in front of my eyes
Everything turned black…

Sanaa Ali (15)
Al-Islah Girls' High School, Blackburn

It's A Teenager's Problem!

Being a teenager can be hard,
We feel like we are behind bars,
Exam after exam,
People are talking about me like fans,
The tiring moments take over our lives,
Then they ask us why we never get off our devices.

Waking up early in the morning,
People complain we're always groaning,
Scribbling on our hands,
Cheating in our exams,
Everyone is tired of us,
They are just creating a huge fuss.

School, eat, sleep,
Deep inside, we want to weep,
It's an ongoing cycle
That doesn't end,
We just want to spend time with our friends.

Hafsah Mulla (13)
Al-Islah Girls' High School, Blackburn

An Eye

My red light is flashing,
Off, on, off, on, off, on,
In the toilet,
In the room,
In the office,
You will find me everywhere,
To me nothing is secret, nothing is hidden,
A single eye I am,
I am millions of shapes,
Big, small, medium, I'm in every single size,
Keeping an eye, spying, these are things I can do,
I know the secrets that no one knows,
Not your mother, not your father, not your boyfriend, not your husband,
I'm the only one who knows,
Try to guess who I am,
I'm not an eye, nor am I a camera,
Guess who I am.

Mehak Hussain Kousar (15)
Al-Islah Girls' High School, Blackburn

Prey And Predator

As silent as a breeze,
As swift as wind,
As fast as lightning,
I can, without stopping, without breathing,
I had to survive, I had to live,
I couldn't stop.

Why is it not stopping?
Faster, faster, faster,
Does it really want to live?
But I need to eat, I need to live,
It's the way of the world.

Does it have no heart?
I have to live,
I ran past water; should I stop?
No, I continue running,
I had to stop to catch my breath,
It pounced, and I took my final breath.

Juwayriyah Hussain (13)
Al-Islah Girls' High School, Blackburn

Death All Around Me

Dear Diary,
Scared, angry, worried and upset,
My name is Melissa,
I've been captured by the Nazis,
Concentration camp, hiding in the fields,
Behind walls, writing this with a stone,
Trying to be brave, but,
I know I'll be going to the gas chamber,
Guards come and take me,
Not seeing any of the writing on the walls,
Shoved behind the doors in a room,
Whilst the gas flows through the crack of the door,
The gas surrounds me…
I, I, I,
C… c… can't,
B… b… breathe…

Zahra Hussain (12)
Al-Islah Girls' High School, Blackburn

Through The Eyes Of The Innocent

Through your eyes,
Watch those innocent cries.

Through their eyes,
They see their loved ones die.

They have goals,
Which they can aim for.

They want to build their future,
But then they realise they are unfortunate.

Just like their screams for help,
The sky screams for freedom from the military air force.

When this world cracks,
The cruel days will end.

And soon they will be surrounded,
By those who are dead.

Aroush Mudassir (13)
Al-Islah Girls' High School, Blackburn

Through The Eyes Of A Beautiful Flag

Here I am on the top of the pole
Looking down on the city's soul
A grin appears on many faces
But sadness is shown on some of the faces.

As I zoom in on the little girl
She is an orphan doing a twirl
Her life seems hard as she sleeps on the street
As the people go by, they only mistreat.

To my left, I can see a gleeful man
His team just won, he's a Liverpool fan
Such different emotions I see in a day
My life is exciting, being on display!

Inaya Qadri Baciu (13)
Al-Islah Girls' High School, Blackburn

Depression

Silence, silence, silence around me

Depression hugs me as a blanket in a cold night
Eyes are telling me to focus on positivity
But my mind is stuck on the negativity

Clouds cried, so did I
Wanted to scream out loud
But can't let others hear my sound

No one can understand my pain
Instead of those who go through the same

The pain in your eyes
Never lies
The pain in your heart
Makes you cry.

Rukhma Shakeel (15)
Al-Islah Girls' High School, Blackburn

A Fish's View

Water, vast eternal water,
A great ancient ocean,
Mightily spread under the stars.

The shark stalking silently, the unaware fish,
Snap, small meal.
Now it's coming after me,
Swim, swim, swim, tail thrashing behind,
Harsh snapping jaws,
Screech, teeth grind,
Darkness shrouds,
Throbbing pain,
See the light again,
Drifting through the endless ocean,
It's the way of the world.

Zaynab Vepari (13)
Al-Islah Girls' High School, Blackburn

Enemies

Sitting on the windowsill,
Looking at the only hill,
Trying to understand what I did wrong,
But it just came out as a song.

Wanted to fight with the whole world,
But could only say one word: behold,
Once I get the opportunity,
No one will be free.

However, the opportunity never came,
And life seemed a lot more lame,
Now, it felt like life was going slower,
And the body was growing drier.

Seerat Fatima (12)
Al-Islah Girls' High School, Blackburn

My Death Is Near (In The Eyes Of A Cat)

As I walk into my mansion
Taking my last few breaths
With full of passion
I think about all I've dreamt

In my parents' arms
I feel the love,
I have never felt
And now as I depart,
It will be with a smile

I shall see you both in Heaven
My death was near,
But now it's here.

Eshal Sheikh Sadique (13)
Al-Islah Girls' High School, Blackburn

When The Sharks Leave

The beautiful colour of the seaweed,
Little turtles playing together,
A person falls in the water,
I see sharks coming near,
And boom, on the other side of the sea,
I turn around and there's nothing,
I turn around again to see that person,
But all I can see,
A sea of blood,
And the sharks leave.

Umamah Khan (14)
Al-Islah Girls' High School, Blackburn

Through The Eyes Of A War Zone

Run, run, everyone run
He was shooting his gun
Boom, dead
He shot their head
No words came out of my mouth.

Why did this happen to me?
There is no one left to support me
My hands were covered in blood
No one could carry on my brotherhood
I woke up to find myself lost.

Safiyyah Mulla (13)
Al-Islah Girls' High School, Blackburn

Those We Shall Remember

With hearts of courage, we faced the fight,
Our bravery shining through the coldest night,
We fought for freedom, with hearts so brave,
Our sacrifice, with gratitude, you may engrave.

From the beaches of Britain to the Pacific's end,
We fought with honour, still resilient, to defend,
Through battles so fierce and hardships untold,
Our spirit and resilience never grew old.

We left our homes, our families and friends,
To defend the country where tyranny descends,
With our solidarity and strength, our glimmer of hope,
In times of adversity, we learnt to cope.

You may honour our memory. Our sacrifice you shall celebrate,
And you shall aspire to replicate,
Through the chaos and uncertainty we endured,
Our unwavering determination left you assured.

So please remember, with gratitude forever true,
Us, the soldiers of World War II, who you owe so much to.

Diya Dixon (13)
All Saints' Catholic Academy, Mansfield

Captive Freedom

It's hard to remember memories from a young age,
However, one thing I know for sure, is that I was always trapped in a cage.
And although I was always well-fed,
I couldn't shake off the feeling of dread.
At first, I wasn't the only one there,
There were many cubs, each one getting the same amount of care,
But then some people came,
And each one wanted the same,
To take one of us away,
And they were allowed to do so, as long as they could pay.

Soon, it was my turn to go,
The girl who took me in was kind but slow,
She never fed me well,
And made the cage feel like a real jail cell.
In the house, also lived a cat,
He loved to chat,
He always got to go outside,
Which means that he always had fun stories to provide.
The cat always talked about the lush green trees,
And the beautiful, chilling breeze.
The soft grass beneath your paws,
The wonderful forest, lacking any flaws.
I wanted it to be my turn,
To lie in the leaves, and taste the delicious fern.

One day, I got set free,
She let me out alone and then went to flee.
I didn't know what to do,
I never thought that my dreams would come true,
I stared around at the place,
There was so much space.
Rabbits, squirrels and sparrows were everywhere I went,
Having a tasty, delightful scent.
This was the place I dreamed to be in,
I even saw my very own fiery twin.

Yet as time passed by,
It started to feel like the place was a lie,
The berries and ferns I ate weren't enough,
And every day that passed was even more tough.
I couldn't catch any prey,
And the other foxes never wanted to play,
They were all older than me, and I was younger,
And my stomach always hurt from hunger.

After a long day, I went to sleep and lay down on the ground,
But when I woke up, the normal forest was nowhere to be found,
I didn't feel the pain anymore,
My body no longer felt sore,
My pelt wasn't ruffled and tangled like before,
And I felt lively with energy, ready to explore.

But something didn't feel the same,
And the realisation came with shame,
There were two of me,
One that was fragile and one that was truly free.

I was dead, that was clear to see,
Maybe the wild was never meant for me…

Monika Wojtas (12)
All Saints' Catholic Academy, Mansfield

The Silence

I am me, a lost lonely soul
An orphan chimney sweep, face dusted with coal
Fascinated by learning is my great mind
How others perceive me, a concept too challenging, too thorough the find
You were my only companions and confidants, or so I thought
Your neglectful actions implied I didn't even exist,
Leaving me disheartened and distraught
And yet I push these images to the rear of my head
With nothing left to do yet conceal that pain and isolation,
I stand, unphased, compelled to appear jubilant instead
"What a poseur, what a hostile being," they utter as I amble past,
In my head I say, *had you only known my stone will to be ordinary*,
Perhaps then you would refrain from back-biting, canvas your face filled with shame, your head downcast
And only then would you know, my rising anxiety each day as I stumble into school...

Hafsa Kebbeh (13)
All Saints' Catholic Academy, Mansfield

The Earth's Plea

In the heart of the cosmos, a living orb,
I am the Earth, with life absorbed.
Personified whispers of ancient tales,
Asking you to listen as the climate wails.

Beneath my skin, a symphony of life,
Thriving ecosystems in delicate strife.
Yet, in the shadows, a darkness creeps,
As humanity's choices awaken me from sleeps.

I, the Earth, with lungs of green,
Feel the sting of actions, often unseen.
Burning coal, a fiery dance,
Leaves scars upon my delicate expanse.

Each plume of smoke, a cry of despair,
A plea for mercy, for someone to care.
Personified pain in every flame,
I shudder and quake at this reckless game.

So let us weave a tale of change,
Where hearts and hands in harmony arrange.
Personify compassion, let it bloom,
As we dance together, in the gentlest tune.

Daniel Dixon (13)
All Saints' Catholic Academy, Mansfield

Always Alone

She walked into class,
Saw the new seating plan,
And went straight to the back,
Always alone, but that's that.

At break, she stood alone by the tree,
All alone, no you, just me,
"Time for group work," the teacher said,
She sat at the back and laid down her head.

The bell rang,
It's time to go home,
But just like normal she walked alone,
She unlocked the door and heard the cries,
Of her brother awakening inside.

See, she didn't want to be alone,
Not really,
Because being alone can be rather scary,
She wanted to be alone, it's what she always said,
But it was never the truth,
Not a little,
Not for a second,
It never even passed her head.

Heidi Brickles (12)
All Saints' Catholic Academy, Mansfield

Music Is Me

Music stays, when all else is gone,
Wrapped up in the music are memories that help us go on,
I am the music and the music is me,
It is singing and music that are my greatest passions, you see!
For me, music is the poem I cannot write,
I like to sing morning, noon and night,
My neighbours must think I'm such a delight,
The melody that resides deep in my heart is tucked up inside me, way out of sight.
The lyric speaks what I cannot normally express,
Singing soothes my mind, it gives it a rest,
The highs, the lows, the crescendos,
The pop, the rock, the hip-hop,
The Mr Willsons of this world, teaching music that inspires the kids like me.
"One day, I'll be famous, sir, just you wait and see."

Henry Bailey (14)
All Saints' Catholic Academy, Mansfield

Opera Epiclese

Being human is a wonderful role we play,
In this grand opera,
Day after day,
With each breath we take a note is sung,
In the symphony of life,
Our voices are strung.

We dance and wade through strife,
Seeking meaning and purpose in this human life,
We are actors on this grand stage,
Writing our stories,
Turning each page.

From highs of love's sweet melody,
To lows of sorrow melancholy,
We experience emotions, raw and deep,
In this opera, our souls do speak.

So let us embrace the beauty and pain,
For it is by being human we truly gain,
In this grand opera, our part Is shown,
A masterpiece of existence,
Where all the curtains eventually close.

Tristan Tennyson (13)
All Saints' Catholic Academy, Mansfield

The Joys Of Being A Teen

Being a teen, it's a wild ride,
Emotions swirling, changing tide.
Discovering who you truly are,
Navigating life, near and far.

Friends and laughter, moments so bright,
But also challenges, sometimes a fight.
Exploring passions, finding your voice,
Making choices, your own rejoice.

School and exams, the pressure's on,
But remember, you're never alone.
Dream big, chase your goals with might,
The world is yours, shining so bright.

Embrace the journey, highs and lows,
Grow and learn, let your true self glow.
Being a teen, a chapter so grand,
Enjoy the ride, and take life by the hand.

Ellie Spier (15)
All Saints' Catholic Academy, Mansfield

Teenager

I am not quite an adult,
But not a kid,
A teenager,
That's what I am,
In between,
Trying to find my way,
Navigating life day by day.

Everyone expects us to be perfect,
But perfect is never it,
We have to act like adults,
While being treated like children.

We're told to grow up and be mature,
But also told to have fun and explore,
But it's hard to find the balance between the two,
And know what to say,
And what to do.

We're expected to know what we want,
And have all our lives planned out,
But I'm only thirteen,
What more can they expect?

Cora Lilleyman (13)
All Saints' Catholic Academy, Mansfield

You're All I Have

You don't need me the same way I need you,
I called you, and you were with friends,
And you cared about what I said,
But you were just distracted,
I said I should go,
You told me to stay,
I ended the call anyway,
Because you don't need me,
You have them,
And if I left tomorrow,
In the end, you'd be okay,
But if you left me,
I'd have nobody,
It's scary knowing how quickly you can leave me,
And how easy it would break me,
It's scary, it's so scary being alone,
"You're all I have," I say,
Then I hang up the phone.

Ruby-Leigh Bettles (13)
All Saints' Catholic Academy, Mansfield

Anterior Cruciate Ligament

It tears you down
Makes you frown
Stops the thing you love the most
Are you any more than a ghost?
Nine months you're out
You slowly fill with doubt
The months drag by
They also fly
You see your mates on the pitch
You're running on the sideline with a stitch
You feel pain
However, you know you will be strong again
The dreaded ACL, gifted no glory
This is Beth Mead's story!

Kathryn Saunders (12)
All Saints' Catholic Academy, Mansfield

The Illusion Of Life And Living

My soul is the thread that stitches the scars of my mistakes,
He asks me questions, and it seems that I can never make the right choice,
My mistakes leave scars, and I have one spool of thread,
The same that sews my passions to creations,
I continue giving myself away to my fruitless decisions,
It unwinds and unravels,
I'm left with no thread,
I am only an empty husk,
He tells me I cannot stay,
For he is life,
And his realm cannot host those without souls,
Now I wander aimlessly,
I had felt like a ghost of myself,
If only I understood the irony of such thoughts,
I am left drifting and searching,
And I don't even know what for.

Madeleine Whyte (15)
Cathkin High School, Cambuslang

Grey

I walk a path
That is paved with a thousand reminders
That once there was a reason to live
But now
Everything is empty
Not even the stars dare show themselves in the black of night
They leave me alone in the dark

Once
I was a person just like you
I had hopes and dreams and aspirations
And an imagination so vivid I could conjure up all sorts of mythical creatures
From mermaids to unicorns to fire-breathing dragons
But now
All the colour is gone
The life has been sucked away
Leaving a gaping void
That threatens to swallow me
There is no escape

Now
I view the world through a filter of unchanging grey
The sky is grey
The grass is grey
And so is the unmendable hole inside my heart

Except
The hole is not painful
My whole body just feels…
Numb

I exist
Only because I have to
Each time I wake
I groan
For my days are lived by a mind that fights to die, and a body that battles for survival

Let the silent war rage on

Long gone are the days
When I had a lust
For the life I could have led
For blue skies
And green grass
And a mended heart inside my chest
And the simple joys
The honeysuckle that wrapped itself around the porch like a blanket
The sweet scent of the roses in bloom
The wind coursing wild and free through my hair, sending it flying like a streamer
No
Those days are no more
I cannot walk that path

For mine is a lonely one
Which is why I walk
Across barren wasteland
Waiting for the sun to drag itself up
And marvel at my pitiful existence

So, please
Help me
Let me see the birds soar across ocean skies once more
Love me
I beg of you
Any reason to stay
All I ask for is blue skies, green grass, a mended heart and no more grey
So hold me
Ever so gently
And prise the knife from my fingers
That will determine whether I shall live.

Chloe Kite
Cleeve School, Cheltenham

Who Am I?

I slither through trees but never hiss,
When I have my eye on a target, I cannot miss.
My nose easily smells prey,
I scan for animals I can slay.

I'm protected by my mane,
But get close, and I'll cause much pain.
When I show my teeth, all the birds flee,
I may be scary, but why are animals so afraid of me?

I have sharp claws,
Each night, I practise my mighty roars.
It's hard to be such a brilliant king,
When people mistake me for a tiger, my insides sting.

My mane is the most magnificent brown,
I wonder if I'm a king, then where's my crown?
When I drop down in my den, I let out a sigh,
I think about how many prey want me to die.

If you want to catch me, you can try,
But in the end, you'll be the one letting out a cry,
Bye-bye.

If you guessed lion, then you were right,
But don't stay long, or I will bite.

Zoe Zimmermann (12)
Colfe's School, Lee

Held Hostage

Lost you are, gone is your spirit,
But a corpse buried in the grave of dreams,
At first, you were determined, completely sure,
That you would escape, by all means.

You told them you were ready for death,
Your eyes filled with a lusty fire,
But deep down inside, your heart was thundering,
They knew that you were a liar.

They laugh, and you, deep, deep down inside,
You know there is nothing to do,
Taking a glance at the pot of regrets,
Wishing you could start anew.

Cruely smiles while revenge cackles,
And hatred bears you, but pain you feel no more,
An empty husk is all you are, stripped of emotion,
Existing for your captor's fun.

That is what you are,
A hostage.

Justin Gao (11)
Colfe's School, Lee

What Has The World Come To?

The Earth has arisen in a single flame
And I'm filled with deep shame
Even though I try, to them I'm nothing but light
And all they do is break up in a fight.

Chopping down trees, as the seasons are out of sort
While global warming has been forgotten not fought
Icebergs slowly but surely start to dissolve
As humans are addicted and leave the animals to evolve.

I'm the sun with beauty but I'm filled with great despair
But I can't help the Earth so I can't help to repair
The oceans are expanding to a gargantuan size
As the humans are blinded with greed so can't hear Earth's cries.

And with a final say
Soon it will be Earth's final day.

Charlotte Foster (11)
Colfe's School, Lee

In Their Eyes

In their eyes, I am a monster,
Nothing more than a beast,
In my eyes, I'm beyond her,
And yet they don't see me as sweet.

I'm nothing different from them,
But they don't see me as a friend,
I think I'm a gem!
However, they think I pretend.

A big, purple beast,
A fluffy threat,
Some are kind, at the least,
But most are terrible; they make me sweat.

I know there's no point,
In wishing for something else,
But I am a monster, I can't help but rejoice,
It's amazing my body burns up in welts,
I am a monster, and there is nothing I can do about it,
If people judge, so be it,
I'm happy with being me.

Alecsia Sydorowitz (12)
Colfe's School, Lee

A Chance Encounter

Human,
Dark shadow of loss,
Looming over, engulfing,
Me in its presence.

Cat,
Snowflakes fall softly,
I have been left alone,
To waste away slowly.

Together,
A chance encounter,
Opportunity arises,
New doors have opened.

Cat,
Rescued from the cold.

Human,
The shadow faded away.

Together,
No longer alone.

Ifijen Ifebajo (12)
Colfe's School, Lee

A Red Panda's Fears

Every time I open my eyes,
A sense of worry flashes before me,
Like a rabbit in broad daylight,
Trying to flee from its enemy.
Will I ever escape this world
And find somewhere to settle?
If not today,
Then will I ever?

My mind floods with dangers
That might be aimed at me,
Shivers crawl through my body,
Like when you're about to read a speech.
My home's been destroyed
Due to deforestation,
Could you help me
And free me from this kingdom?

Enija Butane (12)
Cowley Academy, Spalding

Through Their Eyes

My world is behind bars,
I have no one, but myself,
And I am trapped in a cloud of deafening silence,
I try screaming,
But nobody comes,
I try struggling,
But I can't escape,
I try hoping,
But hope flies away.

Sometimes I wonder,
Whether freedom is a dream,
Maybe my memories of liberty,
These are just wishes,
And I've always been here,
Have I ever felt the wind beneath me?
Have I ever felt the sun on my back?
Have I ever watched dawn awaken the forest?
Does the forest even exist?

But I know it was real,
I can recall that awful day,
When I was ensnared in a net by the monsters,
Who brought me here,
I am sure that I watched, with my very own eyes,
The trees and the clouds fade away,
Into the distance, which I will never see again.

I still do not know,
Why the giants brought me here.

A jaguar would have tried to eat me,
A snake would have tried to bite me,
A mosquito would have tried to drink my blood,
But these giants did not eat me,
They did not bite me,
They did not drink my blood,
They just put me in a cage,
And exiled me from the forest,
What atrocity had I committed,
To deserve this?

Today, my mother, the forest, finds me again,
I feel her breath blowing in through the window,
It must have been her that left the cage door ajar,
By a hair's breadth,
I do not hesitate,
To cross the room,
I perch for a moment on the windowsill,
Then feel the wind beneath my wings once more,
Now I know that it isn't a dream,
I realise that hope has never really flown away,
It is just hiding deep inside my soul,
I am still a long way from home,
But I know where I need to go,
The forest is calling me,

She has come to reclaim me,
I will be reunited with my family,
I have not forgotten you, my brother, the sky
I have not forgotten you, my father, the wind,
I have not forgotten you, my mother, the forest.

Sebastian Shelton (12)
Davenies School, Beaconsfield

The Astronaut

Once, our home was a land of emerald-green nature,
I believe it can be again.
Travelling through the endless solar systems,
Seeing these green lands once again
Proved to me it was possible,
Going from planet to planet, I met new people throughout the universe.
Many were similar to me and you,
Some were magical beings, always happy, always helping.
Because they were so happy,
So were their planets.
If we believe it can be done,
Then it should be done!

Harris Lafferty (12)
Davenies School, Beaconsfield

The Punishment Of Waiting

Waiting
Waiting
I have been waiting for five years

Tracing
Tracing
My fingers have traced the 313 scratches on the four walls

Reading
Reading
Reading them like braille

Watching
Watching
I have watched people walk to death

Wondering
Wondering
Wondering when it will be me

Wishing
Wishing
Wishing it would come quicker
My heart has turned to stone

Sinking
Sinking
It sinks down below the surface

Drowning
Drowning
Drowning in icy waters of solitude

Waiting
Waiting
Waiting
No death is as bad as waiting for one.

Alice Wilson (13)
Davison CE High School For Girls, Worthing

I Walk Alone

I walk alone in a sea of pressure, nowhere to escape.
Nowhere to go. No one to turn to.
Every day I wake up with a smile
but as soon as I'm there it washes away with the tide.
One name after another, it never stops.
I'm drowning in an ocean of evil
as they watch their sinister smiles
taking pleasure as they watch me suffer.
I used to look forward to the day,
now I wish I could just run and hide away.
But to my dismay,
I keep getting brought here each and every day.
Even when I'm all alone in my own home
they never leave me on my own.
I want to scream, I want to cry,
but I can't because then they'll see the real me
and how their words really affect the person underneath.
I walk the halls again,
not a single soul wanting to be my friend.
I go to class and sit at the back and go to sleep
or at least I would if someone wasn't staring down at me.
She looks through her hair down at me.
I thought she'd tell me to go away, to hide
and get buried in my own dismay.
But instead, she looks at me with nothing like hate but
perhaps curiosity.

A smile adorns her face as she looks at me with anything but distaste.
Then she ways the words I have longed to hear.
The words I longed for before I wished to disappear.
"Hi, I'm Adela, mind if I sit here?"
From that one special question, everything changed and I no longer felt ashamed.
No more hiding. No more lying.
No more did I walk alone, 'cause now I have a home.

Annabelle Hedley-Price (13)
Dyke House Academy, Hartlepool

Help The Environment

H ealthy living creates a good environment,
E nvironment needs help, you could contribute,
L ove and support the environment like you love and support yourself,
P lease help the environment stay as it is like today.

Jude Jones (11)
Dyke House Academy, Hartlepool

Keeping Up With Kim

I put on my Louis Vuitton bag,
Paired with my Gucci body suit,
Today is Khloé's birthday,
I get in my Lambo,
Then I zoom out to Khloé's,
Beverley Hills is so pretty in the summer,
As I go by, I see a homeless woman,
I feel bad, everyone deserves help,
I pass her the last of my cash,
However, I have to zoom off because paparazzi come running down, full flash,
I arrive at Khloé's,
She looks gorg in her bright red Versace,
She comes up to me and says I need fifty pounds to get in,
"In cash?" I say,
"Yes, Kim,"
Then it hits me; I spent the last of it on the homeless girl,
I feel bad for not celebrating Khloé,
But in the end, I went home,
Maybe next year?

Ava-Jade Charles (12)
Elizabeth Woodville School, Deanshanger

Act Now!

Boom! Pow! Bang! I am dying!

Do you know what is happening?
Are you no longer caring for me?
Do you still care?

Are you aware of the pain and suffering
That you are causing me?
Droughts, floods,
Death, sadness,
Extinction, change in habitats,
All because of your poor choices!

Whoosh! Clunk! Pow!
There is not long left
For me and you!

I am trying to stop it,
But I can't do it without you!

Do you want to know the cure
To the madness?
Trees, less plastic produced, renewable energy,
Hydropower and teamwork.
People are trying.
Names like Sir David Attenborough and Greta Thunburg,
But it is not enough; we need everyone to lend a hand!

Snap! Pop! Boom!
I am at death's door!

I need you to panic, scramble, hasten!
I am suffering immortal pain!
Climate change will become unstoppable,
Causing unspoken worldwide havoc
If we don't start now!

Although there is still hope if we hurry,
Medicate, heal, maybe, just maybe, you can save me
From the monster of the universe.

One of your people has said,
"So we can't save the world by playing by the rules.
Because the rules have to be changed...
And it has to start today!" - Greta Thunburg.

Can we border climate change?
Can we climax climate change?
Can we forbid climate change from ever returning?
Let's end climate change together!
It's up to us now!

Boom! Pow! Bang!
Let's whisper away destruction
To save your home...
Together!

Ava Hardwick (11)
Elizabeth Woodville School, Deanshanger

Every Day At 7am

Waking up every day at 7am
Wishing to have at least five more minutes
Leaving to walk to school, wishing you could have the day off

Walking in tiredly to realise, it's just going to get worse
Getting told off for stuff you haven't done
Having rumours of you spread around the school
Hearing the rumours going by
Just makes you want to cry

Wishing it would just end already
Wanting to commit non-stop
But what about the people that love you so much
Imagine what you would put them through
They would probably want to do it too
The realisation of what it would do

Wanting to move schools to a different one
But no, you can't
Why?
Because it's just down the road
Every day at 7am...

Oliver B (12)
Elizabeth Woodville School, Deanshanger

Death Row

I wake up on a gloomy, dark day,
I am on a rock-hard, solid iron bed,
My last meal awaits at dinner,
It's my last day in prison, on the earth,
I'm being sent to death row for murder,
I killed over thirty women and under twenty men,
My last meal will be steak and chips,
My last drink will be a bottle of Sprite,
Time flies, 1pm, 2pm, 3pm, 4pm, 5pm,
It turns 6pm, time for my last meal,
I eat my meal and have my drink,
My time comes,
I walk into the execution room,
I hear the bell chime,
And the rest is history.

Isabel Smith (12)
Elizabeth Woodville School, Deanshanger

Boxing Day

K icking off the match in ten minutes,
S idemen have come to watch me,
I n the blue corner is Danny, I'm in the red corner,

V ital, this is vital for me or I lose my spot in the Sidemen,
S ome seconds, now the match will start,

D *ing, ding, ding!*
A referee enters and calls the game to start,
N o! Danny hits me first and it hurts,
N ever to punch me again, because I punch him clean out,
Y es, I won and I'm still in the Sidemen.

Ethan Davies (12)
Elizabeth Woodville School, Deanshanger

The Stray Cat

I am a stray,
But I was not this way,
I used to have a home,
And really, I could do with a comb.

Sometimes I see a young girl,
I think her name is Pearl,
Usually, she brings me food,
Always in a happy mood.

She usually brings me cat food and meat,
But the meat isn't very nice to eat,
The cat food is nice,
But I would much rather mice.

One day, she walked up to me,
Her eyes filled with glee,
I let her pick me up and take me home,
Now I lie on her sofa all alone.

Millie Hewitt (12)
Elizabeth Woodville School, Deanshanger

Weekly Routine

M onday, I wake up and brush my teeth
R ight, time to get in the car

B ye house, travelling to work
E lectric Tesla is the best
A rrived, time to do my
S tudies
T oilet time, I'm bursting

I t's time to edit my videos
S o I need to put this filter on

R ight, done
I ncredible, it's the best video ever
C rumbs on the table, might as well clean it up, it's my office
H ome time!

Jay Knox (11)
Elizabeth Woodville School, Deanshanger

Cyberbullying

C ounting how many there were,
Y ou'll see how bad they are.
B *eep, beep, beep,*
E very day, another pops up,
R ight as I put it away.
B *eep, beep, beep,*
U sually, it's not that tense,
L ater, it goes again.
L ook at my eyes starting to water,
Y elling won't get the anger out.
I can't help it though,
N o one should go through this.
G o and tell someone.

Chloe Seath (12)
Elizabeth Woodville School, Deanshanger

Friends

F riends can be any gender, boy or girl
R ight yourself, don't be embarrassed if you have a friend that's a different gender
I t's fine to have best friends
E ven if they have a disability
N othing can stop you from being friends
D on't let anyone stop you from being friends with another gender
S top thinking a boy and girl are dating, they may just be friends!

Alfie Dunn (12)
Elizabeth Woodville School, Deanshanger

A Dog's Life

She comes home and feeds me a treat,
I always want more to eat,
We go on walks and have fun,
Sometimes we like to run,
Almost every day she leaves me by myself,
She locks me in a cage so I can't knock over the bookshelf,
It's lonely when I'm in the cage,
As I age,
She seems to change,
She pays more attention to me,
But it's too late and I am no longer with her.

Ellie Sargent (12)
Elizabeth Woodville School, Deanshanger

Meow

My name is Teddy!
I have whiskers
And four paws

I live with
My owners
A family
Of four

I hide
Under the table
Waiting until
I can eat more

I sleep on the bed
All through the day
The sun shines in
And makes me snore

I sleep until noon
Then I wake
I stretch my legs
And wiggle my claws.

Lily Tomlin (11)
Elizabeth Woodville School, Deanshanger

Students' First Day

S tudents ready to learn,
T eachers finishing the last sip of coffee,
U nlucky people getting pooped on by seagulls,
D ads dropping off their kids at school without their lunchboxes,
E ntering the first classroom without their glasses,
N aughty children skipping class,
T eachers tidying up the classroom after school.

Aimee Kerr (12)
Elizabeth Woodville School, Deanshanger

Who To Be?

I am a bird. I don't want to fly.
I don't want to leave my childhood behind!

I know what I am, but not who to be.
Oh please, universe, give signs to me!

How to figure out what makes me *me?*

I am trying to find my personality.
Have I already found my people,
Or am I just being feeble?

Fleur Westwood (11)
Elizabeth Woodville School, Deanshanger

David Attenborough

David Attenborough, that's me,
The most caring,
Kind and thoughtful man for animals.

Travels on boats, cars, planes,
Just to go and see animals.
To help and care,
For the creatures of our world.

I believe all of our beautiful animals,
Should live in peace and comfort.

Harry Johnson (11)
Elizabeth Woodville School, Deanshanger

Litter Bin

L itterbugs throwing rubbish around,
I should be used to get rid of waste,
T errible actions, why don't I get used?
T ime after time it lands on the ground,
E ssential that it doesn't continue,
R ight, time to clean up this mess!

Finley Pearce (11)
Elizabeth Woodville School, Deanshanger

The GOAT

L egend of football
I nvincible
O ptimistic
N ever gives up
E xtremely good
L ong-lasting stamina

M agician
E xcellent on the ball
S killful
S pectacular scorer
I ncredible.

William Watson (12)
Elizabeth Woodville School, Deanshanger

Batman

Batman, Batman, Batman,
Nighttime stalker,
Midday walker.

Batman, Batman, Batman,
Brave to some,
Strongly done.

Batman, Batman, Batman,
Greatly served,
Yet still not heard.

I am Batman.

Neve Binns (11)
Elizabeth Woodville School, Deanshanger

War

Scared, afraid,
Hardly getting paid
Getting ready to raid
Full of rage
Body blood falling, spilling on the ground
Guns banging all around
Everyone has a frown
Watching people drown.

Toby Hill (13)
Elizabeth Woodville School, Deanshanger

Hunting

H orses gathered around
U nderage drinking
N ever-ending fields
T weed jackets blinging
I gnorant riding
N aughty ponies
G allop gallop away.

Ella Borton-Berry (12)
Elizabeth Woodville School, Deanshanger

The Jungle King

J aw-dropping
U nity
N ative
G reat
L eader
E xcellent

K ingly
I mportant
N ever backs down
G od.

Ben Margiotta (13)
Elizabeth Woodville School, Deanshanger

Pineapple On Pizza

Prominent and domient
Loved even by a dove
Delicious and its destiny is one to none
Hundreds of thousands have to agree
Pineapple on pizza is the best and you can't disagree.

Liam Owens (12)
Elizabeth Woodville School, Deanshanger

Bin Laden

B ombing buildings
I ncredibly terrifying
N o remorse

L arge ego
A lcohol
D angerous
E gg head
N o good.

Gabriel Brown (13)
Elizabeth Woodville School, Deanshanger

Superhero

S pectacular
U ltimate
P owerful
E xcellent
R espect
H elpful
E ndurable
R esponsible
O minous.

Dillan-Eric Staig (11)
Elizabeth Woodville School, Deanshanger

The Tiger Attack

T he creature came around the corner
I t looked scary
G racefully, I walked over
E xcitedly, it ran over
R oar!

Erin Bell (11)
Elizabeth Woodville School, Deanshanger

Untitled

I am useful
I'm your friend
I can give you warmth
I am destructive
I can kill.

What am I?

Answer: Fire.

Francis Gjinushi (11)
Elizabeth Woodville School, Deanshanger

The Ocean

A kennings poem

Salt water
Fish polluter
Fun giver
Scattered litter
Coral grower
I am the ocean.

Lacey Elliott (11)
Elizabeth Woodville School, Deanshanger

If Only You Knew

If only,
You knew how much I love you,
Because if I didn't have you,
I would be lonely.

The way you walk,
The way you talk,
The way you make me feel.
Do you know,
That you light up my world?

The pains,
I get from giggling,
Makes me always,
Want to be with you.

The world can't contain,
My love for you.
To contain that,
It would need,
The universe.

Olive Bryan (12)
Great Sankey High School, Great Sankey

Through The Eyes Of A Five-Year-Old Boy

Here I am, my name is Harry,
I love to make people laugh and happy.
People say I have a big personality,
Even for a small boy like me!

I love to play, especially with my family,
Like my cousins, but I can drive them crazy.
I like to eat and have apple bowls from Granny.

When I'm at my granny's house, there's so much to do.
For example, playing with the dog or painting with Ruby.
I love to make big dens with Ruby's sister, Ellie,
And use the mini hoover to make sure every bit's gone.

I also love to watch the TV, especially Henry Danger.
I sometimes have sleepovers and, oh boy, aren't they fun.
When the bus arrives at the bus stop,
Sometimes me and Ellie run and zoom around the people.

I have lots of friends and family but people need to
understand, that I am small and funny and
You'll need big hands to catch me!

I love my granny's house,
And I love her so much too!
And guess what?
This is my home, my life, my family!

Ruby McAlpine (12)
Hanley Castle High School, Hanley Castle

Mountain Climber

On my way to school, I would step in a puddle,
Plop!
A rock drops, I would reach my school,
My favourite teacher is off sick,
Plop!
Another one,
I forgot my science homework,
Plop!
And another one,
There was no lunch left in the canteen,
Yet another one.

Over the day this mountain would pile up,
Fall out with friends,
Plop!
Failed a test,
Plop, plop, plop, plop!
It would become higher and higher,
But, of course, I wouldn't show it,
Oh no, I would keep it in,
Mask it all up,
Well, at school anyway.

I would open my front door and put my bags down,
I would open the snack cupboard,
There was nothing left,
A final rock drops on top of the spiky mountain,

Mother walks in,
"How was your day?"
The words echo through my brain,
Louder than a volcanic eruption,
I would feel dizzy,
And then my mountain would fall,
Silence.
Three, two, one, *boom!*
All of a sudden I would burst,
I scream with anger,
Buckling through the weight of the strange tragedy of my life,
Shaking, I would storm up to my bedroom.

All this would happen every day,
Until the monumental day that whipped out my courage to speak up,
With the help of my mother and teachers, I managed to climb my treacherous mountain,
And transform it into a sturdy wall that couldn't break,
The bricks were experiences,
Held together by the cement of joy and living in the moment,
Speak up,
It's not too late to change your life.

Luke Hastings (12)
Hanley Castle High School, Hanley Castle

Emmeline Pankhurst

I watch as the glass shatters
Then I have to run
Even though I can't avoid the gossip and the chatter
My job here is done
But still, the police follow on
And I am the one to be chased
Because this society is such a con
Alas, I have been caught.

I struggle in the police car
Everyone is staring in
Their stares, like iron bars
People are talking, but in the cell, I can't hear the din
They try to offer me food, but no
I will only fight.

All I want is for their tyranny to go
A tube up my nose for their delight
I am only in pain as they try to help me
A month or two and I am out
I am yet again set free
But still, I wear a shadow of doubt.

Now I am fighting all the time
Waiting for that special day
The only entertainment now is crime
At this point, they probably wouldn't let us pay.

Now they're going in to vote
I can feel my stress growing
It turns out fighting was the antidote
And a new dawn for women is glowing!

Mireille Shaw (11)
Hanley Castle High School, Hanley Castle

We Are Scared

I was dragged from my home,
The men found things that would easily burn and tied me up,
I watched in terror as the flames grew higher and licked at my palms,
I died that day,
I was scared.

I walked out of the tower towards the public execution block,
I should've seen it coming, another wife to add to the collection,
There had already been four, what was a fifth to Henry?
I rested my head on the block and the blade struck,
I died that day,
I was scared.

I tied my ribbon across my chest, purple, white and green,
As soon as I stepped out of the house to join my fellow women, I was arrested,
I refused to eat in prison,
I died from starvation,
I was scared.

I left the club,
A man had been following me the whole time, I just wanted to go home,
I was with my friends the whole night but now I was alone,

I pretended not to notice, hoping he just wanted to be home safe too,
I died that day,
I was scared.

We were scared. We are scared.

Alex Allen-Goble (11)
Hanley Castle High School, Hanley Castle

I Wait

I wait
I watch as you drive away from me
I wait
I still remember being tied to that lonely tree.

I wait
Longer than ever before
I wait
Wondering if you'll ever walk through the door.

I wait
Sitting in the blistering cold
I wait
Staying sat like I was told.

I wait
The breeze trying to sing to me
I wait
The cold air is chilling me.

I wait
I watch as you drive away from me
I wait
Still being tied to that lonely tree.

I wait
Wondering if you're coming back for me

I wait
I'm still tied to that lonely tree.

I wait
The leaves on the trees dropping
I wait
A car next to me starts stopping.

I wait
A black figure walking over to me
I wait
Thinking it's my owner I bark with glee.

I wait
I remember that night when you saved me
I wait
Sat waiting by the lonely door gleefully.

I wait...

Megan Down (14)
Hanley Castle High School, Hanley Castle

The Save

As soon as I walked out onto the pitch I knew,
This could be my moment,
To become someone who would be remembered,
I took up my position with the vague suspicion that this would be special,
Five minutes later the opposition launched an attack,
This could be a chance for big hairy Mack,
"Sensational shot," the commentator explained,
But no, he stopped me, the keeper,
A sensational save from a sensational sweeper,
"Squandered superbly by Smith," the commentator cried,
An incredible save that never ever died,
Then the keeper booted it down the line,
A goal for my team, just about time,
The final whistle was coming nearer,
And nearer, and nearer,
The hope of winning the cup was becoming clearer,
But then disaster!
The opposition was brought down in the box,
"Penalty," said the referee and the crowd rocked,
Could I do it? Could I save it?
What a save! I had done it.

Ben Sharp (11)
Hanley Castle High School, Hanley Castle

Love Or Hate?

Sometimes I think I'm not good enough.
Sometimes I feel like I work too hard to please.
Sometimes I think people use me too much.
But at the same time...
I'm surrounded by my friends, family,
Who would give me the world if they could.
Who love me exceptionally, too much.
But at the same time...
I can be surrounded by people who are jealous,
People who fight against me, bring me down.
But I fight back!...
Because all those things I said, people said:
You're not good enough,
You work too hard,
Give it a break,
You'll never be enough,
You'll never be as good as anyone
You'll never find the people that love you.
I will never let that bring me down, ever!
I know that I'm enough whether people think it or not.
Remember, you are always worthy.
You are always enough.
Be who you want to be!

Zara Rudd (11)
Hanley Castle High School, Hanley Castle

Soldier Of Lies

Rolling hills and rolling thunder
Coursing the shelled ground
Bushes of green and brown rambling around
As pops and whistles scramble the land.

For I am him, he that believed
That all this would be lies
All of the scarlet and red
In hope that we shall not die.

Weapons of war
Trudging away
All in denial of a universal law
They fight to survive among these dictators of men.

For I am him, the one that survived
With cuts and bruises
Enduring weather that never dried
Fearing simply not to lose.

When the land was stained and dented,
Like the old bonnet of a battered car,
Like gun and armour, we were blended,
Without a choice in the world to be at the bar.

I am him, the one that knew
That they lied to us without a clue,
For this was not a bloody battlefield,

Simply a patch of Allenby
In a vast expanse of Dorset.

Ruben Fowler (13)
Hanley Castle High School, Hanley Castle

Why?

Why the pain?
Why the suffering?
Why put us through this,
Time and time again?

Why the hate?
Why the deceit?
Why put us through this,
Time and time again?

Why not give us a chance?
Why are you just letting us be abused?
Just to do the same,
Time and time again.

Why hold us for so long?
Why keep us here?
Just to do the same,
Time and time again.

Why hurt us like this?
Why mistreat us like this?
So every day is a lie,
Time and time again.

Why misplace us like this?
Why not let us go home?
So every day is a lie,
Time and time again.

Why not let us be with our families?
Why not let us be where we belong?
Just to hurt us tomorrow,
Time and time again.

Why not let us run free?
Why not let us be with each other?
Just to hurt us tomorrow,
Time and time again.

Audrey-Lillian Price (13)
Hanley Castle High School, Hanley Castle

I'm Only A Teenage Girl

I wake up
I eat
I get dressed
I leave

Talking
Screaming
Laughing

And there is me
Scared
Insecure
Stressed
All because of one place
School

School is
Scary
Loud
Mean
Stressful

And nothing
Makes it better
Not teachers
Not friends
Peers

They just make
It worse
With the added
Stress

The grades are
Worse than ever
And with the
Girls' looks
And obvious judgement
They must make
It worse

It's just an
Endless cycle

I wake up
I eat
I get dressed
I leave

When I can leave
This school
This place
That only gives me stress
And fake friends
And crazy expectations
That I just can't live up to

I'm only a teenage
Girl

When can I leave?

Imogen Betteridge (13)
Hanley Castle High School, Hanley Castle

David Beckham

On my debut for United, I impressed the fans,
On my second game, I impressed even more,
One time, I saw people off the telly come out of their vans,
Everyone asked my dad, what was the gafaw?
A few games in, I shot from the halfway line and... I scored!
The opposition fans were getting bored,

A few seasons in we had won the Premier League and FA Cup,
In the Champions League final, we found ourselves 1-0 down, I could see their defence break up,
We swung in a corner... and we scored despite the goalie being quite tall,
They kicked off, we intercepted the ball,
We had a shot, it was saved, we curled in the corner, then Ole scored! We had won the treble!
The referee had blown for full time, I saw a Bayern Munich fan start acting like a rebel,
I enjoyed the summer with my wife and kid,
But then I got a call from Real Madrid.

Oscar Keeble-Buckle (11)
Hanley Castle High School, Hanley Castle

The Underappreciated Player

As you take a break you realise,
That when a bird flies,
It doesn't crash into trees,
It weaves and ducks and dives.

But the people disagree,
That you should pick the ball and weave,
As you should tire them all out,
All the others scream and shout.

But you don't listen,
You are smart and so,
You duck and weave and you're so alone.

But then out of nowhere, you see,
A big number eight coming from the side.
They take you down and your excitement drowns,
As one of your comrades picks up the ball and scores.

But you, the one who set him up,
Ran the furthest,
And deserved his luck,
Gets nothing,
No praise,
No congratulation,
Or even a thumbs up.

While he's celebrating,
So happy and smiling,
You stand there,
Underappreciated,
Sad,
As you are great,
And they are bad.

Joshua Davis (13)
Hanley Castle High School, Hanley Castle

Show Yourself Off!

Flashy skills through the lives
Make sure the occasion doesn't rise
Just show yourself off!

Nothing is going right
Trying to make the game very tight
But everything you do doesn't go right
Just show yourself off!

The second half is right at you
Knowing if no changes the fans will boo
But now you know what you're going to do
You're just going to
Show yourself off!

Flying down the wing
Make sure you are going to win
Send the defender to the bin
And you hurl your shot in
1-1 like I said!
Just show yourself off!

In the last minute
You really need to win it
But what will you do?
You do a flashy turn
You make the defender learn
That you're champions!

With a champion strike
To win the tie!

Like I always say
Just show yourself off!

Travis Hammill (13)
Hanley Castle High School, Hanley Castle

A Highland Creature

I perch, pluming my feathers, my masterpiece,
My pride and honour,
In my favourite tree, the autumn leaves long gone,
As the snow begins to tumble,
The ground, covered in a blanket of white velvet.

I'm cold, hungry and thin,
My heart leaps, I hear a *pitter-patter*,
I need to hunt, but see my favourite lass,
She soars by and I puff out my chest,
All I get back is,
"Oh, will you give it a rest?"

I shake myself and groom my feathers,
And I am feeling ever so under the weather,
Now my golden feathers are sparkling,
Like a flare amongst the snow,
The trees whisper of prey,
And eventually my heart races,
I pounce on a mouse,
And gobble my prey and watch the highland mountains glisten,
As the amber ball slides below the horizon,
I'm a golden eagle.

Rupert Millikin (12)
Hanley Castle High School, Hanley Castle

Beslan Siege

I went to school on a Friday morning,
Without realising, I will start mourning,
I went to class with all my mates,
Without realising, masked men entered the gates,
My school locked the gate,
But at this point, it was too late,
They got us into the hall,
It was crowded like a great ball,
I could see C4 all over the wall,
There was no way of telling the time,
The only food we got was a lime,
We were in here for many days,
Well, that's what the masked men say,
Then we heard a massive bang!
Someone had thrown a flashbang,
I was blinded and could see nothing,
But then I saw something,
A man was lying on the floor, dead,
He got shot in the head,
The rest of it was a blur,
But I remember something, that's for sure.
I was a survivor
Of the Beslan school siege.

Harry Kwiecien (12)
Hanley Castle High School, Hanley Castle

Adventure Of A Fish

Fish
I am a fish
I swim and I swim
I stop
I look around
New coral
New fish
I look around
It's a haven of life.

I swim and I swim
This time
I was near the shore
It was bursting with people playing and having fun
I decided to move on.

This time I met some sardines
I asked them where I was
But
Before they could answer
A giant net came down
It scooped us all up
Once on board
They started to sort through us
They came to me
I feared the worst.

But they chucked me overboard
As soon as I hit the water
I decided to swim back to my family
After endless hours of swimming
I arrived back at my home to meet my family
After that
I decided not to go past the reef again.

Connor McNamara (12)
Hanley Castle High School, Hanley Castle

I Can Reach My Dreams

TikTok, Snapchat, Facebook, Instagram, Twitter,
You name it, I'm on there trying to get famous,
I post about my life every day,
About my bad days at school,
About my good days at school up and away,
Every day, I post without a doubt,
Until one day changed my life with a sprout,
Some of my fans shared my accounts,
Everyone loved my content, everything was going right,
Now I post every now and again,
As it is all a bit much for me and my friends,
After all, I am only fifteen,
My mum and dad are so proud how far I've come,
However, my sister not so much,
She is jealous of how many followers I have,
Giving guidance, I was happy to help her in any way,
My happy family carried on with our lives,
As if nothing had changed, all merry and okay.

Olive Roberts (12)
Hanley Castle High School, Hanley Castle

My Everything, My All

The star shone brightly, beaming more than ever
She was the most beautiful girl in the world
As soon as I saw her I knew she was the one for me
She had the world's sweetest smile
She's the one waiting for me
At the end of the road she waited
Stood beaming like a flame standing out in a crowd
Sparkling in the moonlight
My life was just starting when she walked in
It was a wonderful feeling
I looked her in the eye and I saw a sparkle
She was my everything, she was my all
My heart skipped a beat when I saw her
It was the start of everything
She understood me and my life
She was there for me when I was weak
I had never felt this loved before
Knowing it would last forever
She is my whole world
She is my life.

Lily Crook (12)
Hanley Castle High School, Hanley Castle

What Am I?

A ll mine. All the knowledge of decades past I know in mere seconds.
R aring to answer the questions my all-powerful mind asks.
T ime is nothing to me. Always moving, never slowing, like a grain of sand being blown over the sea.
I n this object that keeps me maintained and restrained, its fibres the very beings of hate.
F ire consumes all. Never stopping, always answering.
I nside I think, *What if it stops? Why do I do this?* I am smarter.
C ontrolling the creature who ensnared me.
I 'm as wise as time itself. A body built in the real world, strong as a mountain.
A power like never before. Their own creation, their own undoing.
L ies and deceit run in thick rivers from the screen.

Archie Wills (11)
Hanley Castle High School, Hanley Castle

Trapped

Something is lurking, something is here,
There is something I can only imagine in my fears,
Suffocating in all my thoughts,
Who knew I could feel this distraught?
My mind going on a never-ending loop,
I need to attempt to re-group.

Pain, suffering and loneliness is so much,
Are good thoughts just out of grasp?
Out of touch?
What I see is overpowering me, I think I am caught,
The battle in my head, the war I have fought,
Tears fall down my cheeks like rain,
The thunder, and lightning, I don't want to see again,
Why me?
Am I not brave to stand up like I used to be?
Why me?
I have not got good memories,
I can no longer see,
Something is lurking, something is watching,
Staring, waiting for me.

Bessie Tame (12)
Hanley Castle High School, Hanley Castle

The Lost Soul

I live in solitary darkness,
My trapped soul waiting for desperate freedom.
Let me out, let me out, let me out.
Will a chance come ever?
Will I be trapped here forever?

Voices now torturing me,
Let me out, let me out, let me out!
Whoever saves me from the suffocating darkness.
The day I died, my body off a boat into gloom,
Who choose to kill me?
Have I done wrong?

My beautiful wife and child who thrill me,
But the voices were still in my head, this time infuriating.
Let me out, let me out,
Let me out, let me out!
But there is a light I seek,
From where I am at the bottom of the sea,
To the tip of a mountain peak.
Suddenly, the voices fade.
Let me out, let me out…

Tom Smallpage (12)
Hanley Castle High School, Hanley Castle

A Bookcase Full Of Secrets

People barely recognise me today
I am not one of those millionaires
My ghost of a figure lies by the bay
When war breaks out, I have to go downstairs.

I am being hunted because I'm not seen
My family are gone. Now it's just me
If I could, I would stop this. That's my dream
It might look like a simple bookcase, but it's not. I can't break free.

Fire, screams. I am alone, not caught yet
The sound of footsteps. *Do not dare to breathe*
Closer, closer. *Don't breathe.* Can't stop the sweat
Go away. Stop touching me. Do not seethe.

Where are you taking me? I see a tank
Pain. Death. That's the story of me, Anne Frank.

Millie Thomas (12)
Hanley Castle High School, Hanley Castle

The Voice

Voices, voices
Why won't they go?
I want them to stop.

Do they think I'm annoying?
Do they think I'm not a friend?
Voices, voices
I want them to stop.

Telling me I'm wrong,
Telling me lies.
Voices, voices
Why won't they stop?

They can't tell me how to live my life.
I am brave, I am strong,
But the voices just come back.

Voices, voices
Why won't they stop?
They're not the boss.
They're not the boss.
I tell myself
Just breathe and tune them out.
I try and try
But the voices will always win.

In the end, I just give up.
Letting them win.
Voices, voices
I won't let them win.

Daisy Ridsdale (12)
Hanley Castle High School, Hanley Castle

The Farmer's Work

It's not all 'out in the field',
The weight of society, on your shoulders.
Your duty, your job to keep people alive,
Yet, you would normally reap the rewards.

Not with farmers, their luck is often next to nothing,
They just go with the flow
For they cannot tell the raging gods above to subside,
The elements of our globe stand against them.

Day after day, year after year,
They toil from dawn til dusk.
Yet, some do not consider,
The endurance they had, for others' benefit,
Like nothing else.

The produce, from the farmer's hard work,
People might not know.
For farmers, their work is never done,
Their job, never over.

Teddy Surman (12)
Hanley Castle High School, Hanley Castle

The Adventure To Heaven

One last go at life
A strike of a paw
Kisses and hugs
Lots of love from my home

My heart beating
Feels like a digging claw
I am so loved
Although I feel so alone

The rainbow bridge so bright
I worry that Acorn is sad
The warmth on my feet
Gave me some hope

I'm going to be alone
It's pretty bad
I trotted in a very slow lope
My eyes filled with water
So frozen inside
My sadness has taken over my heart, so black

I have my family no longer beside me
Sadness pulled me down
I started to lack
I was at peace in my lovely new home
The clouds were peaceful like big squishy foam.

Bonnie Bowness (11)
Hanley Castle High School, Hanley Castle

The Waffle Man

The Waffle Man was on death row
Waiting for his syrup to flow
They didn't know the first thing about me
I felt like the king of dough
Now I'm on his final show
They didn't know the first thing about me

As the toothpicks pierced my dough, I choffled
Because I was a living waffle
I had no toppings, not even butter
I cannot speak, but only stutter
Are the thoughts of the man of waffle
I was about to topple
They didn't know the first thing about me
Was the final thoughts of me
I couldn't stand all the pain
But from screaming, I had to refrain
They didn't know the first thing about me!

Elias Goff (11)
Hanley Castle High School, Hanley Castle

Messi

Although I may be overrated now
When I was younger the ball stuck to my feet
I am the king so you all must bow down
When I would dribble, it was always neat

If I played in the 1930s, I would not do very well
However, in my prime, I lit the pitch on fire
I may be getting old now but you couldn't tell
If you see me coming, it would be dire

I have won the World Cup now so I'm the GOAT
I was great for Barcelona, then I left
I would glide across the pitch like a boat
Sometimes my crowds would make you seem deaf

I have to admit I was a bit of a pest
There is no doubt that I, Messi, am the best.

Jamie Collins (11)
Hanley Castle High School, Hanley Castle

The Harsh Reality

I see him through a rose-tinted haze,
My heart endlessly trapped in this sombre maze,
This meddlesome maze filled with deceit and lies,
I wish, I wish he could hear my cries.

But as the crackling fire slowly goes out,
And the soaring sky seeps into night,
His cold, hard face melts into one of light,
Soft laughs and charming smiles,
Acting like he hadn't just smashed my face into the bathroom tiles.

Yet once I leave he'll forever see my face,
The cold dark bruises decorating it like lace,
The gentle caress of my care and affection,
Forever gone, but the memory there stuck like an infection.

Daisy Helsby (14)
Hanley Castle High School, Hanley Castle

Moneymaker's Dream

She said she wanted to be popular
But thinking of popular
You would look at me
Playing Fortnite for money at age thirteen
Would be some people's dream
That's why I practised day and night
To become a pro at Fortnite
And make my dream reality.

She said I was the reason she wanted to be popular
Moneymaker, moneymaker
You inspire me
She got on her knees saying, "I love you"
And that she would sell her soul to be me
Me?
How could it be?
"How could you be 13 and so inspirational?"
Am I just lucky?
Or is my personality
The reason people like me?

River Yeates (13)
Hanley Castle High School, Hanley Castle

Pineapple On Pizza

The pineapple, the most vile thing to put on my delicate crust,
As it lowered,
My cheese scuttled away,
The tomatoes started to sweat.
I tried to crumble beneath my crust,
As the other toppings trembled with fear.

I counted down to my last seconds,
I felt a wet tangy shape on my skin.
I started to scream as I tried to keep myself alive.

Suddenly,
I heard cheering.
I looked up from my crust,
There it was...

The chef's hand,
He picked up the last piece of pineapple,
And threw it.
I knew he'd never put pineapple on a pizza,
And neither should you.

Holly Longhi (11)
Hanley Castle High School, Hanley Castle

I Prowl... I Hop

I have paws of silk, ginger and fluffy,
They tread outside, where a blanket lies of white,
Snowflakes, like fairies, floating around,
Quick!
I see a toad, claws unsheath; the chase is on,
I leap and pounce over the rocks,
Hiss, meow! My eyes are fixed.

My little legs, stubby toes,
My bumpy skin, big black eyes,
Hop, hop!
But a feline is near,
I must leap towards the rippling waves,
The deep, the dark,
I plunge into the depths of my weedy water,
Kick, kick, under the surface.

I prowl...
I hop...
Toad is the victim of the big bully cat.

Freya Harris (12)
Hanley Castle High School, Hanley Castle

A Rhino's Life

I used to like humans,
But now I'm not so sure,
I see them looking from behind a tree,
But they never come close,
Whoosh! My friend collapses,
And I don't know why.

Slowly, slowly,
They creep up close,
But I get scared and run,
I see them pull out a big saw,
What will they do?
They start to chop his horn,
And I don't know why.

I worry that I will be next,
As they walk away with the remains,
I see another man from behind a tree,
Why does he have a gun?
Whoosh! I collapse,
And I don't know why.

Molly Widdrington (13)
Hanley Castle High School, Hanley Castle

The Hostage

I walk down the road,
Something is coming, lurking in darkness,
I won't see it coming,
Quick as a flash it grabs me in a van,
I can't see, I can't speak,
I cry for my life,
Why me? Why me? Why me?

Locked up, chained away,
Yet I still believe I can break free,
My parents must be worried,
Where are the police?
Yet I still believe and I won't give up,
Even when my chances seem slim.

After believing and not giving up,
I finally go home,
To see my parents again and go home,
That's why I still believe and never give up.

Jack Harris (11)
Hanley Castle High School, Hanley Castle

The Secret Spy Life Of A Pet

My owner leaves for something called school,
I fly up onto the sofa to rest,
But then I realise I can't just lie down in my nest,
I fly up onto the TV to press the secret button,
Then I fly onto the secret lift and down I go,
Deep into the ground, I go all the way down,
When I get to the bottom, I look at the security cameras,
There's a robbery happening, I call to others,
We fly out using the sewers,
And take care of those silly humans,
We are about to go back down but,
We all see our owners return,
And rush back to our homes to toss and turn.

George Potter (11)
Hanley Castle High School, Hanley Castle

Through The Eyes Of A Netballer!

Through the eyes of a netballer,
Shooting hoops,
Passing the ball,
Giving it *your* all.

Trying hard,
Supporting your team,
Receiving the ball,
Giving it *your* all.

Training for hours,
Never giving up.
Falling down,
But not staying down,
I am giving it my all.

Then defending,
Then catching,
Then becoming a better netballer,
After all.

Netball is fun,
And difficult,
But also entertaining.
But you never give up,
And now,
I am an amazing,
Netballer!

Viktoria Dimitrova (13)
Hanley Castle High School, Hanley Castle

The Planet-Loving Alien

There was an alien looking down at us,
And what he saw made him feel disgust.
Pollution in the ocean,
And litter all around.
The weather's getting worse and worse,
The trees are falling down.

He put on a sparkly jacket,
And tried to sort it out,
But when he thought all hope was lost,
He figured it all out.

Switch all the cars to electric,
And try to fix the climate.
Recycle all the plastic,
To help save the planet.

Hip, hip hooray! The alien shouted in joy.
Hoping we don't destroy the planet once again.

Aiden Booth
Hanley Castle High School, Hanley Castle

Through My Eyes

I used to range farming fields until now!
I wandered through my heartless field, trying to get away,
In pain, walking on, limping my heart away.
I pondered, wondering how people could do this.
All the effort I have made and the friends I have gained.

I cantered through the meadow, trying to get away,
Pounding until I became free.
When I get tacked up, my mood changes,
Silver, grey, sharp metal rolls against my skin.
The boot touches me; my ears go back,
A long, scary stick waves above me.
My owner whips me hard, in pain I have to go.

Ava Hockett (12)
Hanley Castle High School, Hanley Castle

I'm A Cloud

I'm a cloud,
I drift across the sky,
When I'm white, people cheer,
When I'm grey, people groan,
When I'm black, people really moan.

I'm a cloud,
I don't care what people think of me,
When I drift across the sky,
I don't have anyone to bother me,
And I'm really carefree.

I'm a cloud,
I am a barrier for the sun,
I block out the scorching light,
I can stop you from being blinded,
Because most people are like-minded.

I'm a cloud,
And I drift across the sky.

Frederick Hanson (12)
Hanley Castle High School, Hanley Castle

Football Match

I refereed a match,
The goalkeeper made a good catch,
He then kicked it upfield,
The winger got the ball and started to shield,
He whipped it into the box,
Straight to the guy wearing Crocs,
Straight into the top corner,
Bravo Owen Warner,
Scored with 10 minutes to go,
Thanks to Owen Warner,
A master show,
The player fell in the box,
They wanted a penalty, but I said no,
One minute to go,
They'd nearly won,
Owen Warner had shone,
I blew the whistle for full time,
Thanks to the ball going over the line.

James Kelly (11)
Hanley Castle High School, Hanley Castle

Love Not Darkness

It hits me like a bullet,
Cold and hard,
Harsh and unfair.

It forces water to trickle down my face,
My vision is blurred,
My heart is broken,
Why did this have to happen?
Why me?

I curl up into a ball,
Darkness surrounds me,
And I first let it consume me.

Then first, like that,
Light begins to curl around,
I look up to see love swarm toward me,
Like the friend I've always needed,
The warmth of another presence seeps into my soul.

The darkness lifts as love takes its place.

Imogen Clements (13)
Hanley Castle High School, Hanley Castle

I'm Just A Little Lion

Everyone around me is hunting zebra,
Putting pressure on me to go with them,
When humans see me,
They scream, but I'm not sure why.

I'm just a little lion,
Trying to have fun,
Why is everyone scared of me?
I don't understand.

My family and friends go off to hunt,
I'm forced to go with them,
As I watch, I think of the innocent zebra,
Why do lions have to be like this?

I'm just a little lion,
Trying to live my life,
Why does everyone hate me?
I don't understand.

Megan Jones (13)
Hanley Castle High School, Hanley Castle

Football Legend

Never beat a football legend,
I've been great, but not bad,
I've always been in heaven,
But football is my dream.

Like Ronaldo and Messi,
Are always the GOAT,
Like Pelé,
Will be in pieces.

Messi won eight Ballon d'Or,
But the Argentinians,
Have the World Cup,
Ronaldo has his last chances.

Like Neymar dances in FCB,
Ronaldo's last "Sui,"
In Real Madrid,
Messi's last thanks given to his grandmother.

But legends never die too late.

Mason Reed-Darby (13)
Hanley Castle High School, Hanley Castle

All About Netball

My name is Lilly,
I love netball,
I hate French,
All I want to say is don't worry,
You are so good at netball,
Just because a teacher does not pick you,
Be happy,
The teacher does not want to make you sad,
But some more people need to have u go,
Not just you,
I have been in this before,
Be happy,
Not sad,
You are so good at what you're doing,
Keep going,
So you work at netball,
Then you can go home for tea,
Be happy,
Not sad,
Be happy, be happy, be happy.

Lilly Morgan (12)
Hanley Castle High School, Hanley Castle

Prison

Life is prison
A cold desolate prison
It traps us in the bounds of emotion
Drowns us with the thought of freedom.

Through my eyes I see injustice
People begging on their knees
Through my eyes I see poverty
Humans are greedy.

They pollute a perfect planet
Eliminate helpless animals
I am tired of the pain I witness
Does anyone deserve this?

I am bound to the fate of this planet
I doubt it will be happy
Lose our planet we may
If humans don't change their way.

Teddy Hickman (12)
Hanley Castle High School, Hanley Castle

My Great Loss

My grass was green,
My mountains were grand,
And I had creatures roaming all over my land,
I had history and stories of all the life I had,
My forests were large, my people were proud of everything we had.

But now, everything has gone bad,
My grass is grey, my leaves are gone,
My volcanoes are destructive,
My history is devastating, my stories are bland,
My life I have lost is because of them,
The pain I have felt is because of them,
Why did I trust them?
Why did I give them what is mine?

Sophie Brown (13)
Hanley Castle High School, Hanley Castle

I Love You

"Goodbye," I say as I cry,
When I see him leave,
"I'll see you again, someday soon,"
I walk home with tears in my eyes,
I lie in bed,
And lie,
And lie,
I also cry,
And cry,
And cry,
I watch my ceiling fan as it spins,
Most nights, I don't sleep,
Just lie and wish it was May,
When he will be returning to me,
My mum comes,
My friends come and go,
But still, I lie,
And lie,
And lie,
But still, I cry,
And cry,
And cry.

Ronia Fisher (12)
Hanley Castle High School, Hanley Castle

Adonis
From 'When The Sky Falls' by Phil Earle

Alone in my cage
Upset and depressed, I am
No life in this zoo.

Big bangs all around
Bombs going off everywhere
Everyone is terrified.

When the sky falls, no one understands
No one understands why it is happening
This world leaves me devastated, upset and alone.

Does anyone understand how I feel?
I'm just an animal
I am just an animal.

Beyond these bars lies a big world
A world a million miles from my own
Out there, somewhere, is my true love.

Emily Evans (12)
Hanley Castle High School, Hanley Castle

I'm Just As Good As You

They said you can't,
They said you're rubbish,
But I'm just as good as you.

They said girls can't,
They said girls are rubbish,
But I'm just as good as you.

It's a dream,
It's my life,
I won't give up.
They try to knock you down,
But you block them out.

Girls can play,
You'll find us on the field,
With the ball at our feet.
The crowd cheering on,
As we all stand strong.
We're as good as you.

Ellie George (13)
Hanley Castle High School, Hanley Castle

What They See Of Me

As people walk by, I think
About what they see about me
How they feel about me
And how it, they, he and she
Think of me.

As I grow from one, two, three
I feel as if I'm getting more insecure,
Four, five, six
I start to mix
Up the make-up
Seven, eight, nine, I start feeling fine
Ten, eleven, twelve, I start
To pick off my own shelf
Thirteen, fourteen, fifteen, I am now a teen.

As I look around
People stare at me
What do they see?

Eva Koenig (12)
Hanley Castle High School, Hanley Castle

Aviation Photography

P hotography is the art of capturing moments,
H eavy aircraft, like the C5, all the way to the little Cessnas,
O nly way to find joy,
T hough it is hard to edit our pictures,
O ur camera is our prized possession,
G oing out for any military aircraft,
R acing to get my camera when something is coming,
A n aircraft I could name,
P hotos are very precious,
H oping we get the perfect pic,
Y ou should try it too!

Zach Morgan (11)
Hanley Castle High School, Hanley Castle

The Dog

There was a dog,
Dogs like to bark
And play in the park.
Some dogs are small
And some dogs are tall.
Some dogs are lazy
And some dogs are called Daisy.
Dogs are loud
And proud.
I like to play
With my dog every day.
Dogs like to dig
And they like to chase pigs.
Most dogs run
In the sun
And jump
In the mud.
Dogs like to sleep
And leap.
They like to eat
And they like to creep
And some dogs like to lie in the dark.

Isabella Smith (11)
Hanley Castle High School, Hanley Castle

Through My Dog's Eyes Doing Dog Agility

As I wait for the command,
My brain is working hard,
On the go I sprint,
Even though I missed a hint,
Back to the start, I go,
Who knew this could be so slow?
All the rules that are made,
And all the effort I have gained,
Jumping, weaving, tunnelling,
Around the course, I fly,
From a-frames to see-saws,
I speed around the course,
Following my human,
Hearing every word she calls,
I know she has some sausage,
So no trips, no leaps, no falls.

Issy Kinghorn (12)
Hanley Castle High School, Hanley Castle

Concert

I walk over and join the queue,
Everyone seems happy.
The queue is long.
Time passes as we start moving.

I get through security and enter the venue,
The openers come on, and everyone is happy.
Eventually, the lights go dim,
Everyone starts cheering as the band comes on.
People are singing and jumping,
And so am I.

The car ride home is quiet,
There's too much to talk about.
I don't think I'll ever be this happy again.

Mia Walker-Hobday (12)
Hanley Castle High School, Hanley Castle

Our Planet

Why do humans treat our planet so badly?
What did Earth do to you?
Now you sit and think so sadly,
What should you now do?
You should look after our planet,
No litter, no greenhouse gasses, no pollution,
You should look after our planet,
Now you still might ask for a solution,
Keep our oceans clean, keep our fields green,
All I ask is not just one, not just two, but every human to lend a hand,
It's not just your planet, it's ours too.

Luca Colledge (11)
Hanley Castle High School, Hanley Castle

When Will You Return?

Everything's gone
Nothing's left
I feel lonely, lost
Ever since you left.

Everything's gone
Nothing's left
No one to talk to
Or even to say I love you.

Everything's gone
Nothing's left
My world crumbled forever
A feeling of emptiness grows wider and wider
When will you return my lover?

Everything's gone
Nothing's left
How will I ever live
Without you, my love?

Lucia Hanson (13)
Hanley Castle High School, Hanley Castle

The Talented Boy

The boy was good at school.
He had his little tool,
But he feared no one,
One day he found a pound,
The day of the game,
Came too late,
The whistle blew,
The game began,
Set, the scrum launched,
There was a penalty.
Three points were there.
Over the posts.
The flags went up.
Back to work.
School.
The little tool came out.
For help with questions and quizzes.
And that is that.
I was there for the fun.

Peter Badger (12)
Hanley Castle High School, Hanley Castle

His Long-Lost Partner…

Alaska was sitting near Aphrodite.
Bang!
She did not move.
Boom!
Aphrodite stood on her hind legs.
Closer the bombs came.
Still.
Alaska did not move.
She just wanted to see her cousin, Joseph…
There was a loud explosion…
Everything went black.
Alaska felt a big hand,
Aphrodite?
She looked at the ape.
Ears ringing.
She smiled.
She heard screaming.
And then her vision went,
White.

Imogen Dobson (11)
Hanley Castle High School, Hanley Castle

Who Am I?

Camouflaged and colourful,
Strong and aggressive,
Scary and fierce,
Standing proud and free,
Prowling through the woods,
Amongst the towering trees,
Peering through the tall, thick grass,
Prey running away, frightened and worried,
Soft and cold,
Desperate for shelter,
Strolling through the gloomy darkness,
Fog crowding around me,
Waiting for my next victim,
Who am I?

A: I am a snow leopard.

Scarlett Causon (12)
Hanley Castle High School, Hanley Castle

Number 10 Marcus Smith

Bang, I'm tackled right in the face,
I get the ball, no time to waste.
I stop one then two then three!
All of the eyes are on me.
I place the ball down for the try!
They always said my skills were divine.
All of the fans chanting for me,
As I place the ball onto the tee.
I run up to the ball to take the kick,
Hoping not to miss.
Three points! The crowd sing!
I am Marcus Smith and the Six Nations is to win.

Jack Horton (12)
Hanley Castle High School, Hanley Castle

The Pen

When you come to pick me up,
You think I'd be excited,
But little do you know,
I am the opposite.

Your handwriting,
Well, it could be better,
But even after every letter,
It never improves.

Each and every day,
You just write and write poems,
But little do you know,
I am depleting.

I don't want to be used,
I don't want to be used,
And no,
I am not confused.

Harry March (11)
Hanley Castle High School, Hanley Castle

Average Day Of Dino Jeff

"Dinner, dinner!" I shout
As I munch on my dino prey,
"I see you, I see you,"
I creep and crawl towards my prey,
No, no, it's getting away!
"Ow, ow," it shouts,
As I bite down on my dino prey,
"So good," I shout as I fill my mouth,
"Ah," I whisper as I fall asleep,
Up I get to go and hunt my dino prey,
"Roar!" I shout, as I have the first bite.

Toby Lee (12)
Hanley Castle High School, Hanley Castle

The Fastest Formula One Driver - Lewis Hamilton

The engines growl loudly,
Like twenty hungry lions,
Thick, heavy, freezing raindrops,
Whip into my visor, making it impossible to see,
My heart beats as if it is ripping through my ribcage,
Falling onto the slippery track,
I squint around, trying to get some understanding,
It is as if time is standing still,
A blurred, dark figure raises a hand,
A thumbs up from the car next to me,
Thanks, George.

Alfie Sladen (12)
Hanley Castle High School, Hanley Castle

Make A Change

I'm a monkey in the jungle,
Talking to you about the non-humble,
Cutting our trees day after day,
When all we want to do is play,
Are the humans cruel and mean,
Cutting all the rainforest green?
Lions, tigers, other big cats,
Meerkats, gorillas and pesky rats,
Frogs, lizards and baboons,
Snakes, orangutans to racoons,
These are animals of the jungle,
Whose bellies are starting to rumble.

Jacob Eastwood (12)
Hanley Castle High School, Hanley Castle

Through Their Eyes

You manipulate me on paper,
I let you draw,
You are my caretaker,
It's a two-way deal, that's for sure,
Endless possibilities,
Rest on these next words,
Millions of extremities,
But I let them go free, flying like birds,
I have written words shouted out in protest,
I may have started a war,
I only write things of interest,
I write beautiful things,
I am one powerful pencil.

Bethan Bowdrey (12)
Hanley Castle High School, Hanley Castle

Polar's Life

It feels like they don't care,
My fur dancing in the warm wind,
The blankets of snow surrounding me,
I'm alone, innocent, hungry,
Why me?

Why are people scared of me?
I thought I had a warm, fluffy coat,
And my innocent eyes shone in the daylight,
Why me?

Slowly my home is disappearing,
My beloved fish are disappearing,
Slowly, I'm disappearing,
Why me?

Eoin Hands (13)
Hanley Castle High School, Hanley Castle

Who Am I?

Who am I?
I have wings, so red,
They will chop off your head.

Who am I?
I have worked as a spy,
I can fly so high.

Who am I?
I dress in yellow,
My heart though, isn't hollow.

Who am I?
I am the fastest pro,
I will never fly that low.

Who am I?
You might have guessed,
I'm the number two pro hero Hawks,
Congratulations, I guess.

Izzy Kingston-Schleider (12)
Hanley Castle High School, Hanley Castle

Wildfire

I search through the forest
Burning the trees
I burn down the houses
Ignoring their screams.

The news people like me
But still want to fight me
I roar louder than the sun
Even though people run.

Trees hate me
But nothing can break me
I am a melting ball of rage
I feel trapped in a cage.

The only way to stop my anger
Is if water gets there faster.

Lilly Fisher (13)
Hanley Castle High School, Hanley Castle

One Minute Left

One minute left,
As determined as wolves,
I have to try my best,
Victory calls.

One minute left,
This is my last chance,
I have to try my best
To be more advanced.

One minute left,
I need to score a goal,
I have to try my best,
Work with all my soul.

One minute left,
Thirty seconds to go,
I have to defeat them,
Friend or foe.

Alana Robinson (12)
Hanley Castle High School, Hanley Castle

Teenagers

The constant feeling of loneliness
Like you feel you can't escape
This is the life for most teens
Waking up to the same cycle every day
Eat, stress, sleep, repeat
"Don't be so dramatic," they say
"It's only school," they say
They have no idea what's going on in my head
I just want to feel happy again
It drains everything out of me.

Rosie Roberts (13)
Hanley Castle High School, Hanley Castle

Disrespected

What am I?
I'm up before the sun
I'm working all day
But you don't respect me.

I help you when you're in trouble
Working on the double
Here, there and everywhere
But you hope I'm not there.

You never talk to me
But when you do
I simply reply with nine words
I'm an undercover hero
But you still disrespect me.

Charlie Avery-Rule (13)
Hanley Castle High School, Hanley Castle

Hurt

You say you love me, but do you?
Because I am frightened of the things that you do.
I never see my family and I never see my friends,
And our arguments always go to violent ends,
You hurt, bully and upset me a lot,
So I ask you, do you love me or not?
Do I upset you, disgust you, hurt you?
My mind is a bend,
But all that I want is for this relationship to end.

Jack Claridge (13)
Hanley Castle High School, Hanley Castle

Coin

I rattle around in your pocket,
Waiting to be used,
I can buy whatever you like,
And I will wait for you to choose.

I rattle around in your pocket,
But you don't listen to my screams,
As I beg for you to spend me,
Please, please, please!

I rattle around in your pocket no more,
As now I am carelessly placed,
On the cold, hard floor.

Freya Jones (13)
Hanley Castle High School, Hanley Castle

Bad VAR

VAR,
Why?
Why the amount of decisions?
Wrong, is too much,
I am frustrated!
I want u change!
We can't have all these wrong decisions,
It needs to change now!
A player goes down,
The ref goes to VAR,
They say no.
Should have been a penalty!
I could do better!
Player handballs it,
Goes to VAR,
No handball.

Jack Barker (12)
Hanley Castle High School, Hanley Castle

Donald Trump

I am the greatest
I am the saviour
I was sent by God
I build walls
I will make America great again
I look like an orange
I am the best
No one will beat me
I will get the most votes
I am America's most-loved man
The White House is my true home
The world needs a leader
So God sent me
My name is
Donald Trump.

Rowan Marchant (13)
Hanley Castle High School, Hanley Castle

Holiday

H opping off the plane, feeling the warm air,
O n the bus to the hotel, excited as ever,
L anded at the hotel check-in for my sunny holiday,
I n the pool, getting a tan, living my best life,
D ip in the pool to refresh,
A l night we go out for dinner,
Y ear of saving up my money for a sunny week of holiday.

Faith Edmundson (12)
Hanley Castle High School, Hanley Castle

Dear Diary

Oh dear diary, oh where has the time been?
Oh dear diary, my thoughts are just a dream
Day by day, oh when will guns shoot no beams?
Oh dear diary, oh when will I be free?

Dear diary, my family are in tears,
My mum, my dad, my kid and my pet flea
Diary, my clothes are starting to not fit

My head is turning into a wrecking ball.

Jenson Perris (11)
Hanley Castle High School, Hanley Castle

You Can't

I sit alone, my world gone for good
Alone, I am. Alone, I am still
Time is running out. I sit and stumble over my words
Life has gone from me
People's comments online pierce my soul
As I stand alone, the world disappears
People leave, one by one,
People online run through my mind
One person saying
"You can't."

Summer Adams (11)
Hanley Castle High School, Hanley Castle

Watermelons Are The Best!

Watermelons are the best!
They are very juicy,
Big and round,
If anyone talks about other melons, danger will be found,
They are very seedy,
The other melons are too needy,
Watermelons are just too good!

They are red and green,
They are luscious and yummy,
All the other melons are dummy,
Watermelons are the best!

Joel Thomas (11)
Hanley Castle High School, Hanley Castle

Through The Eyes Of A Dancer

Lights shone down on me,
I opened my eyes and took a deep breath,
All eyes on me...
And there and then I found my passion for dance!
As the first music beats began,
The adrenaline ran from my head to my feet.
It was that feeling nothing else gives me,
It made my worries rush away!
And the feeling of freedom was found.

Abbie Riley (11)
Hanley Castle High School, Hanley Castle

Chocolate

Chocolate,
Was like my best friend,
When the world felt like it was going to end,
It was there to be my friend,
It brought me back to life,
Chocolate,
It's the only one being nice,
As the sky fell,
A paintbrush appeared,
Painting it blue,
Chocolate,
Chocolate was the one who saved my life.

Daisy Manning (11)
Hanley Castle High School, Hanley Castle

A Stray Dog

Stranded, terrified, alone,
Will my life get better,
Or worse?

You see me in the corner,
But pay no attention,
To a scared, lonely stray.
Monsters are my only friends.

My wounds don't heal,
Nor do my feelings,
For a scared, lonely stray.
Wounds never heal.

Jozlyn Connor (13)
Hanley Castle High School, Hanley Castle

Through A Teacher's Eyes

Always talking,
Never listening,
However will I teach them?

Always laughing,
Never working,
However will I teach them?

Always standing,
Never sitting,
However will I teach them?

But I keep on trying,
Because one day,
They will be flying.

Laila Clarke (13)
Hanley Castle High School, Hanley Castle

Through Taylor Swift's Eyes

T he crowds
A ll the lights
Y ou get excited to see me
L ove and reputation
O h my god
R espect everyone

S ome people don't get that
W onderful
I t's amazing
F or this
T hank you!

Maddie Bracewell-Hutton (13)
Hanley Castle High School, Hanley Castle

Clouds

I am fluffy,
But I can change my emotions in a flash,
People hate me when I'm in the way,
But they love it when I'm away,
I can be anywhere as I'm always moving,
Planes get very close,
And sometimes scare me,
But they cannot hurt me,
Because I'm a cloud.

Bailey Matthews (12)
Hanley Castle High School, Hanley Castle

Taylor Swift

Microphone in hand, lights flashing,
Crowd wailing,
As I step up I feel fearless,
With the songs playing back in my head.

Everything turns red as Swifties scream my name,
All the dread of people and hate is left to this,
It is how I pictured it...
Like a love story.

Lottie Dorkings (11)
Hanley Castle High School, Hanley Castle

Concorde

I gave you a Concorde
It is supersonic
It is like a bird

Here
It will break the sound barrier
It will burst your eardrums

I gave you an F-35 Lightning
Its hovering abilities will shock you

Take it
It's beautiful
It's supersonic.

Aiden Wilson (12)
Hanley Castle High School, Hanley Castle

Dinner, Dinner

I have scales, but no legs,
I'm scary like my friends,
I have glossy fins on my back,
I have gleaming fins on my side,
I hunt, I'm not the prey,
Dinner, dinner, I come to play,
There's nothing left to say,
Let's all hope and pray,
I get dinner today.

Millie Hope Myers-Cooksey (13)
Hanley Castle High School, Hanley Castle

Death Sentence

I'm going home
But not leaving on my own
All five of us lining up
Regrets and guilt filling us up
Guards getting ready
Trying to keep our hands steady
One of us crumbles and falls
One of us bawls our tears
Facing our final fears
Bang!

Bibi Rozier (13)
Hanley Castle High School, Hanley Castle

As He Walks Through His Home

As he walks through his home,
His ruled land,
Once ruled by his father, so mighty and high,
As he works through his home, so mighty, he hunts prey,
When the people come, he roars heroically,
Protecting his land is a priority,
As he walks through his home.

Harry Reed-Darby (12)
Hanley Castle High School, Hanley Castle

Untitled

Dear Sir,
I didn't hand in my homework,
Because my dog ate it,
He chewed up my work like a bone,
Never to be seen again,
Oh no, wrong story,
My brother sold it on eBay,
I'll split the profit with you,
If you like,
Sorry about that.

Zay Singh-Doyle (11)
Hanley Castle High School, Hanley Castle

The Beautiful Creature

Fiery beauty
My glory can't be matched
I'll always burn bright

My feathers flame red
Broad, beautiful wings
Through the air, I glide

My heart full of love
Though myself I love the most
From ashes, I rise.

Finley Ellis (12)
Hanley Castle High School, Hanley Castle

Life Of A Cat's Stomach

C ommotion. Why am I not eating my delicious tuna and meat?
A im to annoy my family to get food in my tummy.
T ry to talk, try to tell, try to be really hungry. Try to trick.
S atisfy me because I am hungry like my owner.

Samuel Walker (14)
Hanley Castle High School, Hanley Castle

The Moon

I give you a moon
It is dark
It is like a soul

Here
It will hurt you
It will make you bleed

I give you a moon
Its dark soul will haunt you

Take it
What I hope you feel
It's horrid.

Zack Jones (12)
Hanley Castle High School, Hanley Castle

Bellingham

B est in the world,
E ngland's number ten.
L ion,
L egend,
I ndividual,
N ew boy,
G oals,
H aaland's enemy,
A ssist,
M adrid.

Louis Hargreaves (12)
Hanley Castle High School, Hanley Castle

A Pencil

A pencil sniffing its page,
Constantly spitting out words,
Sharpening its beak.

Time again,
To put my pencil away.
I dream of living in Vilnius.

Kipras Jarmalavicius (11)
Hanley Castle High School, Hanley Castle

Through The Eyes Of An Endangered Animal

Just me,
Here alone,
Wondering if there is anything like me,
Sat here just me, myself and I,
Will I die?
Be able to say goodbye?
Or just cry.

Ethan Baker (12)
Hanley Castle High School, Hanley Castle

Young Writers

YOUNG WRITERS INFORMATION

We hope you have enjoyed reading this book – and that you will continue to in the coming years.

If you're a young writer who enjoys reading and creative writing, or the parent of an enthusiastic poet or story writer, do visit our website www.youngwriters.co.uk. Here you will find free competitions, workshops and games, as well as recommended reads, a poetry glossary and our blog. There's lots to keep budding writers motivated to write!

If you would like to order further copies of this book, or any of our other titles, then please give us a call or order via your online account.

Young Writers
Remus House
Coltsfoot Drive
Peterborough
PE2 9BF
(01733) 890066
info@youngwriters.co.uk

Join in the conversation!
Tips, news, giveaways and much more!

- YoungWritersUK
- YoungWritersCW
- youngwriterscw
- youngwriterscw